A GARDEN FOR ORPHEUS

ZT TOSHA

Philosophical fiction

A GARDEN FOR ORPHEUS

ZT TOSHA

From an artistic perspective, we perceive that our thoughts are inherently shaped by material objects, as well as the constraints of time and space. These elements serve as integral components of our cognitive processes, influencing our creative expressions. However, while time and space exert considerable influence over our thoughts, the concept of infinite time and space transcends our sensory perception. Despite being beyond tangible observation, they continue to exert a profound influence on our artistic interpretations and imaginings.

PROLOGUE

Beyond language lies the vast expanse of the unknown. Language, while a powerful tool for communication and cognition, often falls short when faced with the intricate subtleties of existence that defy conventional expression. These ineffable aspects resemble an unsolvable puzzle, defying the constraints of linguistic structures. In moments of silence, when words falter, we grapple with these enigmatic facets of life. We transcend the boundaries of ordinary language and delve into the abstract realms of the mind, emotions, and environment. In this ambiguity, we find solace, acknowledging the inherent limitations of language as we navigate the complexities of existence. Some truths evade linguistic capture, requiring us to draw upon the perspectives and insights of esteemed thinkers to navigate the complexities of emotions and abstract scenarios. Our quest for understanding mirrors the deciphering of life's intricate mosaic, as we strive to unravel its multifaceted structure.

In the face of adversity, our pursuit of truth remains steadfast, enduring the passage of time as we delve deeper into the recesses of our consciousness. Within the depths of our subconscious, we embrace doubt and curiosity, recognizing the seeds of uncertainty that reside within us. Through ongoing introspection, we courageously confront the shadows of our illusions, gradually unveiling the intricate fabric of existence, one revelation at a time. ZT Tosha's reflections poignantly encapsulate the essence of this journey, urging us to embrace the profound mysteries that lie beyond the confines of language.

A GARDEN FOR ORPHEUS

Exploring Consciousness Through Art and Philosophy

"A Garden for Orpheus" transcends mere exhibition and literature; it's a profound journey into the depths of the human psyche. Through the captivating artworks of ZT Tosha, we're drawn into an exploration of consciousness itself. This collection challenges us to contemplate the very essence of our being. Does consciousness originate solely from the physical realm, or does it reach beyond, into realms yet unexplored? Through the symbiotic relationship of art and philosophy, this compilation acts as both a mirror, reflecting our innermost thoughts, and a window, offering glimpses into the realms of the unknown.

Each piece by ZT Tosha serves as a testament to the intricate connection between form and meaning. With vibrant imagery and deep narration, "A Garden for Orpheus" bridges the gap between the abstract and the tangible, making the ineffable graspable to the human mind.

In this captivating book, the boundaries between art, philosophy, and consciousness blur, inviting us to delve into our own existence. "A Garden for Orpheus" isn't just a physical place; it's a state of mind, where the complexities of human experience are laid bare, and where the pursuit of understanding reigns supreme. Within the expansive realm of consciousness studies lies a myriad of questions, challenging conventional wisdom and urging us toward deeper introspection.

Does consciousness solely arise from the physical realm, intricately linked with the workings of the brain, or does it transcend material boundaries, existing as a non-physical entity?

Amidst this sea of inquiries, "A Garden for Orpheus" emerges as a beacon, guiding readers through the intertwining paths of art, science, philosophy, and personal narrative. Through its pages, the essence of the book converges in a profound interplay of artistic expression and philosophical contemplation, delving into the depths of human consciousness and the limitless potential of creativity.

Through curated themes, the book offers readers a measured exploration of the human experience, fostering contemplation and introspection. By blending narrative and visual elements, "A Garden for Orpheus" beckons readers on a journey of self-discovery, prompting reflection on life's mysteries and the boundless capacities of the human spirit.

In questioning the intricate nature of consciousness, this collection serves as a catalyst for dialogue and exploration, igniting curiosity and inviting readers to delve into the profound mysteries that lie at the heart of human existence.

THE INESCAPABLE PRESENCE OF TIME

In the silence of my chamber, illuminated by the light of a modest table lamp, I find myself immersed in deep introspection. The restlessness of the outside world fades, surrendering to the riddle of my existence. Time, that inexorable force, casts its shadow over my consciousness, an ever-present specter that haunts my thoughts. I always feel weighed down by my decisions. They are crossroads, each filling my fateful imagination with possibilities, rewards, and power. Written into the essence of my reality, each twist, failure, and success forces me to deal with the notion of impact, choosing one path and abandoning another. I got rid of one influence by adopting another. Among the myriad strategies, one stands out in particular, Impact influence.

This marks the critical point where fate, as I understand it, turns in the right direction. This influential force demands clarity and conviction and has the potential to make a significant difference. I see personal growth as the core of the hard choices that bring me closer to who I am. Impact influence appears to be a pivotal moment, a stretch where fate hangs in precarious balance. It requires precision and decisiveness and has the transformative power to reshape my social perceptions. The inscription upon my desk, delicately inscribed upon the back of my humble sketchbook, arrests my attention: "For the world to exist, mine must precede it. Each morning, I awaken in the world, and each night, I disappear from it."

A deep enigma it poses, hovering before me like a specter of existential inquiry, summoning me to introspection. In its cryptic origins, it dangles tantalizingly, a mirror reflecting upon my very essence. Thus, once more, I am confronted with the relentless interrogation: "Why am I here?" Within the tangled web of our existence, where the mind intertwines with body and soul, we often make the mistake of assuming that any change in the physical or mental sphere signifies a transformation of consciousness. Yet our own experience testifies to the contrary, confirming that consciousness, that elusive essence, remains unchanged amid the turmoil of our existence. And again as we reflect on our lives, we see that this conscious presence has been ever-present, steadfast, and unyielding. It neither moved, nor manifested, nor disappeared; it stood unchanged over time.

Consciousness, in its essence, is always spontaneous, evolving within its openness, accessible, and visible to the discerning mind. To comprehend the genesis of consciousness, the presence of other consciousnesses, and a novel insight are necessary to grasp its transience. For this "new" consciousness to credibly attest to the departure of the "old" consciousness, it must exist prior to the vanishing of the old consciousness and endure thereafter.

Only under these circumstances could the new consciousness testify to the disappearance of the old consciousness. While all phenomena are subject to beginnings and ends, consciousness transcends such limitations, devoid of a beginning or endpoint. Do we then presume that we vanish along with consciousness?

Upon introspecting our existence, the truth emerges unequivocally: that consciousness, this presence, endures eternally. It doesn't falter, it doesn't shift, it doesn't emerge or dissipate; it remains unchanged throughout the annals of time. Otherwise, a new insight would be required to perceive the loss of consciousness.

In the depths of introspection such as this, I resemble a solitary figure amidst the vastness of my backyard. Time, much like the gentle, meandering course of a tamed river, flows through the vastness of my consciousness, molding and shaping my perception of past days and the ever-evolving present. I maintain with steadfast determination that the future eludes our reach, a mere semblance veiled amid the shadow of uncertainty. Tomorrow lingers like a distant specter, while all events unfold within the endless flow of today's continuum. Seeing consciousness is akin to reaching for an inaccessible shadow, mysterious but undeniably authentic. I guess I'll never really know the truth. It's the not knowing that keeps me going. Even if I never find out the secret, there's something kind of comforting about having one. It's like... it gives me hope or something. Ignorance or lack of knowledge can sometimes bring comfort or hope. I may never uncover the truth, but I find solace in the possibility that there is something unknown to me.

This unknown element, whether it's a secret or a truth, provides a sense of intrigue or mystery that adds value or contentment to my life. In essence, it reflects the idea that uncertainty can sometimes be preferable to absolute knowledge. As time marches forward, I feel compelled to embrace its relentless movement.

It is a quest towards self-awareness, a decisive, crystalline truth that allows my consciousness to illuminate the labyrinth of existence.

It assumes the guise of a silent mentor, who invites me not into the abyss, but into a realm deep in self-discovery and enlightenment.

However, consciousness, similar to the eternal stars scattered across the night sky, retains its unchanging singularity and transcends the limits of external perception. I yearn for comfort, but life's enigmatic riddles persist in their inscrutability. Entering the realm of self-awareness serves as a poignant reminder of the deep beauty within us, the core of our consciousness, which transcends the limits of time and space. It reflects the breadth of human experience. Unless my mind distorts or alters my perception of the external world, there is a deep connection between my mental state and the external reality around me. Deep within my mind, my mental life reflects a significant part of the complexity of the external world. Here, in my mind, everything, from the deepest emotions to seemingly remote places, is woven wonderfully into the fabric of my mental system.

My own experiences have been a jar, a mirror through which I see the world around me. My mental space inherently holds complex psychological associations that shape my outlook on life. So my focus is in the realm that characterizes these supposedly inevitable overlays. The venue holds an interesting appeal for me. Rarely do transcendental, clear facts offer Kant's notion of "ding en sich."

Transparency masks are more like a menacing barrier, perhaps equivalent to a superskull.

Modern physics, exemplified by its belief in collapse found in quantum mechanics, supports the idea that the ancient worlds were purely mental and that the interconnectedness of the universe, originating from the smallest atom up to a superstar is evident. In the interplay between modern physics, especially the enigmatic principles of quantum mechanics, and ancient theories that posit the fundamentally mental nature of the universe, I find myself at the juncture of exploration and contemplation. The interconnectedness that permeates existence, from the quantum world to the cosmic scale, hints at a deeper truth about the nature of reality – the enigmatic symbiosis of particles and waves, consciousness, and matter. At the heart of this framework lies the essence of communication: the self, an entity that transcends the limits of individuality. Like countless flavors of saltiness, the self defies neat categorization, its essence unfolding in a symphony of experiences. As consciousness expands, it converges into a unified state, transcending the boundaries of separate identities. The essence of all communication, the self, lies at the center of this complex web.

Even the self, like taste, has non-specific elements and saltiness; there is no such distinction between inner and outer, the accumulation of multiple intelligences.

Once sustained, individual consciousness expands, creating a unified state without separate or exceptional consciousness. Time remains eternal, constant, and unchanging. It flows quickly, unaffected by circumstances or events.

Time is the immutable course of events, the center of the essence of life. Time, with its rhythmic cadence, guides my research, revealing the fleeting and ephemeral essence of life.

In this cosmic game, I am just a humble observer, trying to unravel the mysteries of existence and consciousness, one fleeting moment at a time.

ARCHITECTS OF WISDOM

In the constant search for enlightenment, the ever-changing contours of our understanding collide amid the cosmic order of experimentation, where the changing paradigms born of the revelations of science collide. The empirical certainties we grasp are revealed as ephemeral specters, whose substance fades as we face the prospect of change or the looming bustle of undiscovered truths. We find ourselves in a sea of uncertainty, questioning the very foundations on which we walk. Empirical truths, gleaned from the crucible of direct observation and experience, stand as sentinels guarding the threshold of the enigmatic depths of nature's mysteries. Yet even as we peer through this portal, we encounter obstacles, impassable boundaries where the ethereal essence of consciousness eludes our grasp, inviting us to embrace alternative ways of understanding. The vertical ascent of experiential knowledge offers a balance, assuring us that amid the tumultuous currents of existence, nature maintains its unchanging essence. Within the echinoid forms, with their sinuous contours and intricate designs, we glimpse the unfolding discoveries that await our discovery. The nexus of human experience, which includes thoughts, emotions, and the interplay of souls, eludes the boundaries of empirical research, eluding tangible understanding. In the field of mathematics, where abstraction intertwines with reality, we embark on a journey of conceptual exploration.

The mysterious laws of arithmetic, illustrated by the subtraction of one from one to produce zero ($1 - 1 = 0$), highlight the intricate dance between empirical understanding and intuitive insight. Through tangible examples, we unravel the enigmatic union of numbers and sets, laying the foundation stone on which the edifice of mathematical enlightenment is built.But mathematics is not only a tool of technological progress; it is the crucible in which the abilities of reason, problem-solving, and critical analysis are forged. Just as mathematical puzzles require evidence to solve, so claims of the supernatural must be subjected to scrutiny and validation, lest they dissolve like fog in the glare of empirical research. Thus, in our quest for wisdom, we are walking the labyrinthine corridors of human understanding, guided by the flickering torch of empirical research and the intuitive whisper of personal insight. In this symbiosis, we find not only the keys to unlocking the mysteries of existence but also the enlightenment that will guide us through the shadows of uncertainty.

Personal beliefs, inherently subjective, require transparent support and evidence for their powerful claims. Encouraging individuals to "bare their reasoning" ensures accountability and protects against the influence of unverified statements on others.

Science, with its methodical journey through observation, hypothesis, experimentation, and data examination, stands as the lone path that provides evidence-based truths, free from personal bias and subjective interpretation. Although faith can provide comfort, only the scientific method satisfies the hunger for objective, reliable understanding. While empirical observations hold fidelity, they also attract the specter of misinterpretation, advocating humility and receptivity.

Frameworks that proclaim absolute truths lose credibility with the influx of fresh insights, requiring periodic recalibration, withdrawal, or outright rejection. While empirical understanding alone fails to capture the depth and complexity of the human odyssey, insight transcends factual boundaries, embracing a broader spectrum. Insight involves not only the collection of data but also the skillful application of understanding with insight and empathy, enabling sound judgment shaped by experience, intuition, and compassion.

The limitations of empirical understanding stem from its reliance on observation, measurement, and analysis of specific phenomena. In contrast, human experience encompasses subjective and intersubjective realms that elude easy quantification or objective examination. In essence, while empirical understanding proves useful in understanding certain aspects of human maturation, it only proves inadequate in understanding the intricacies of human existence.

However, empirical understanding, when intertwined with personal experience, feelings, and cultural acumen, enriches our understanding of the intricacies of human existence. Existence takes place within the parameters, constants, and laws that govern the cosmos. Consequently, anything that shapes the functionality of the universe allows creatures akin to us to thrive within it.

These truths may seem rudimentary and obvious. If the universe made beings like us physically implausible, our existence would be impossible. In an anti-intellectual universe, observers like us would not be able to survive.

Our existence is tangible. Being here, actively engaged in observing the universe, signifies our sustainability within it, intertwined with its essence, suggesting that we originate from the universe and are intrinsically interconnected.

As the annals of human societies unfold across the epochs, we find ourselves entwined with concepts that resonate among the diverse species inhabiting our planet. Yet, an enduring question looms, casting its shadow over the chronicles of our being: why does humanity reign supreme over the world, surpassing the strength of lions or the majesty of whales?

The immutable truth of power and privilege permeates our reality, shaping our perceptions and guiding our lives. Stripped of the privileges, whether technological or societal, that adorn our existence, we confront the stark insignificance of our being. A singular trait emerges, setting humanity apart from the throngs of creatures that populate the earth: our inherent inclination towards cooperation.

This intrinsic quality has propelled us towards the realization of aspirations far beyond the reach of our counterparts. While cooperation exists among our fellow denizens of the wild, their organizational structures pale in comparison, bound by rigidity. Ants scuttle, bees hum, monkeys swing, and wolves howl in unison, yet their collective endeavors falter before the grandeur of human enterprise. The scale serves as the pivot for our triumphs, reflecting the values coursing through our collective consciousness, shaped by our sheer numbers. Humanity stands unique, unbound by rigid constraints that hinder collective action.

Our unparalleled capacity to bond and cooperate with strangers navigates the intricacies of human relationships with unmatched fluidity. This cooperative trait empowers us to make wise judgments, transcending limitations that confine lesser species. This ability allows us to collaborate within vast networks, pursue diverse goals, and exhibit prudence in adversity, shaping our evolutionary path. Yet, amidst our successes, an enigma persists, veiling the origins of consciousness in mystery. What truths lie beneath our existence, and what do they portend for humanity's future ?

Death has become such a fear for humankind today. To win, one must ensure that there is no gap between one's past and present, no matter what. Associating the past with the present implies an unconscious expectation that that identity will expand in the future. It is necessary that "everything remains the same" on a personal and social level to prevent destruction and death. An unfortunate misunderstanding occurs when it is realized that the "old" was beneficial for some and harmful for others. Thus, some frantically defend the continuity of experience, while others demand the destruction of any continuity, forgetting that the person will be absurdly deprived of their freedom. So, the idea of death in religious and spiritual traditions follows from their dogmas; therefore, dogma, when presented as an unquestionable truth, leads to obscurantism and ignorance of what is a natural and inevitable event. All the famous revolutionaries of the world share Prometheus' pride but also his courage to actively oppose Moira, the goddess of destiny.

Morality is the law of self-constitution. There is a fierce struggle within and among men.

As he is crucified between the affirmation of his identity and the identity of the world, the self-proclaimed master of heaven and earth who, through denying death, attempts to create a new identity by accepting it, exalts himself as the only one who is capable of destroying one world and creating a new one. There is a turning point in human history, and he has a choice to make. A choice that is becoming increasingly free and personal. Nature teaches us that the universal order - as we have known it - is cyclical; everything in life is cyclical from birth to death. In the evolution of human thought, phenomena have always existed, but our perceptions, understanding, and interpretations of them have changed.

When a human being dies, their biological processes cease, marking a crucial phase in the natural cycle of evolution.

This event entails the dissolution of one's identity and the initiation of various transformative processes. As far as we can tell, our bodies are made up of the same chemical elements as far-off nebulae, and our actions are governed by the same universal laws. The subjective content of our experience changes constantly. Despite the many changes we experience externally or that we create for ourselves, the essence of our personality remains the same. Throughout life, our essence, our core, to which we have given various names from time immemorial, gives us a strange assurance and certainty that our Self, or subject, in a wide range of feelings, perceptions, images, and acts, remains virtually identical. Interestingly, this sense of identity is stronger and more stable if a person experiences more frequent and intense internal and external changes. As if these changes are a condition for the stability of this feeling.

The eternal duration of the core in man and the experience of his permanence, his stability, and his immutability, and the world with all its changes, fast or slow, are perceived as something essentially identical to itself.

Something unique, something that is within yourself. It is man's code, the Authentic Self. Is our perception of identity, both of ourselves as invisible subjects and as objective realities, illusory? In that case, does it serve a purpose important to human existence? Do things not constantly change around us, do personal and world catastrophes occur, haven't entire continents disappeared in the past, and isn't man dying? Man has learned to defend himself against threats from within by denial, renunciation, and rationalization. We might ask how man reacts when confronted with mutations of historical events that require a "reversal of all values." The world is coming to the end of another war, and people are struggling to maintain a sense of identity. Discontinuity in the world and life is a constant source of fear and threat for humans. We strive not only to restore individual continuity but also social and historical continuity.

Ah, the future of humanity, a grand mural painted upon the wall of our collective destiny, unfurls before our eyes, suspended between the weight of our choices and the loftiness of our aspirations. In this vast theater of existence, where the players tread upon the stage of time, we are tasked with a solemn duty, to confront the immutable truths that lie at the heart of our being. It is in embracing compassion, that tender flame flickering within the depths of the human soul, that we find the strength to face the trials that beset us.

Through wisdom, garnered from the crucible of experience and introspection, we may discern the paths that lead us toward enlightenment and understanding.

Collaboration, that harmonious symphony of minds and hearts, serves as our beacon amidst the tumultuous seas of change. Together, we navigate the treacherous waters of environmental peril, striving to safeguard the fragile balance of nature against the ravages of our own making. Technological marvels, born of human ingenuity, hold the promise of a brighter tomorrow, yet they also beckon us toward the precipice of uncertainty.

It is in our pursuit of technological advancement that we must tread with caution, lest our creations outpace our capacity for wisdom and stewardship. Social justice, that elusive ideal for which we yearn, demands our unwavering commitment to equality, dignity, and human rights. In the face of oppression and injustice, we stand as guardians of the downtrodden, champions of the marginalized, and custodians of a more just and equitable world.

And amidst the shadows that linger at the edge of existence, we confront the specter of existential risks, those ominous portents that loom on the horizon, casting their long shadow upon the fate of humanity. It is in acknowledging these perils that we find the resolve to confront them, to defy the darkness with the light of our collective resilience and determination. In cultivating a deeper understanding of ourselves and our place in the universe, we commence upon a quest of self-discovery and enlightenment, a pilgrimage of the soul towards its ultimate destination.

And it is therein, in the crucible of our shared humanity, that we discover the truest expression of our highest aspirations and values, forging a future illuminated by the radiance of our shared humanity. Human will has no purpose other than to support consciousness. Support must be disciplined, and creation is the most effective source of patience and clarity. The act of creation is a persistent rebellion against human life, requiring daily efforts, self-control, strength, and asceticism to achieve the seemingly impossible. Ironic thoughts prompt passionate actions. A thought that rejects unity glorifies diversity. Not anarchy, but harmonious diversity of beauty is the essence of art. If the circle is a symbol of the equally beautiful, then the square is a symbol of the unequally beautiful. A person's destiny can be shaped by their creativity if they are free to rebel, be diverse, and make a difference.

Sisyphus is an absurd hero living in an absurd world. His contempt for the gods, his hatred of death, and his passion for life cost him unspeakable punishment. He invests his whole being to achieve nothing. As Sisyphus descends again and again down the slope and approaches his rock, he is then stronger than his rock and superior to his fate. The myth of Sisyphus is only tragic if the protagonist is aware of it. A proletarian among the gods. Given his miserable situation as he descends the precipice, he is aware of the full weight of his impotence and revolt. While the insight must torment him, it also completes his victory. Happiness and absurdity come from the same place. No fate is covered with contempt. Sisyphus' heart is darkened by the memory of earthly moments.

Amid a desolate and empty world without a master, Sisyphus is happy. He realizes that every speck of his stone, every mineral flash on that night-filled mountain is his world. His world is special and his destiny is his own, unique and unrepeatable. He knows that he is the master of his life.

The Underground Man, struggles with the absurdity of human existence and the pursuit of happiness. His rambling and introspective monologues shed light on the inner questions and contradictions inherent in the human condition. Here is an excerpt from "Notes from the Underground" that touches on the intertwined aspects of happiness and absurdity: "Man is sometimes strangely, passionately, in love with suffering... Man is afraid of himself... Man likes to make roads and create... but, on the other hand, he likes to create obstacles and destroy." .. Of course, he is aware of his own absurdity... But all the same, he will never get rid of his absurdity while he is human". Dostoyevsky captures the paradoxical nature of human desires and behavior, emphasizing the simultaneous pursuit of happiness and tendency toward the absurd. In the human experience there is a deep connection and interplay between opposing forces: a delicate balance between light and dark, joy and sorrow, clarity and confusion. Within this game, the essential duality of human consciousness is born. Imagine a moment in your personal life where happiness and absurdity coexist, where moments of pleasure mingle with the irrationality of life, revealing the inherent complexity of existence. In this arena, moral absolutes fade into ambiguity, challenging our perceptions of right and wrong.

The contrast between good and evil, positivity and negativity, reverberates through human consciousness, shaping our understanding of virtue and vice. Like a pendulum swinging between extremes, our emotions fluctuate between elation and despair, reflecting the nuanced nature of the human condition. Time, the eternal interaction of past and future, shapes our sense of identity and purpose. Memories intertwine with aspirations, leading us through a journey of self-discovery and growth.In our existence, inherent duality remains a fundamental aspect of our reality, encouraging contemplation and introspection. Accepting the complexity of human nature, whether we like it or not, we move through life, searching for meaning and understanding in the midst of uncertainty.

VULNERABLE CLARITY

Imagine a handful of perfect sand. If it is scattered before one, can one see the first, second, or fiftieth grain? Like grains of sand, individual seconds are nearly indistinguishable from each other. They have similar qualities and characteristics that make them compatible and interchangeable. Whereas the unconscious mind has no inherent qualities to distinguish one second from another, practically speaking, each second is a perfect moment with the same structure as any other. This simple illustration reveals an interesting aspect of time. Given time in isolation and the lack of external cues, it is difficult to assign a specific schedule to the events. Periods do not have inherent signs or differences. To make sense of time, we create systems such as clocks, calendars, and measurement systems that help us organize and quantify the passage of time by creating a sense of order and progression in seemingly impossible categories to remove the difference. It provides a framework for measuring and tracking the development of events and facilitates understanding of our experiences and interactions with the world. Without this conceptual framework, individual moments in time would remain unequal and confused, making it difficult to form a coherent chronology.

In physics, time is the cornerstone of our understanding of the universe. It plays an important role in the dynamics of physical systems and the flow of events. Even in physics, the concept of time can pose serious problems. One example of this is the concept of time inequality, which is embedded in some laws of physics.

In phenomena such as the laws of motion, the equations describing the behavior of objects during rotation do not change.

This means that the laws of physics do not take the direction of time, emphasizing the role of time in the complexity of physics. Physically only, this means that there is no inherent "arrow of time" that distinguishes the past from the future. Each moment appears to be coherent and indistinguishable from the others. Another example is the theory of relativity, especially the phenomenon of time dilation. According to this theory, factors such as velocity and gravity can affect the passage of time. For example, if two observers move at different speeds relative to each other, they perceive time differently. This means that the time lapse is not absolute but depends on the observer's frame of reference.

The relativistic nature of time introduces new complexities to our understanding of its sequence and evolution. In philosophy, the nature of time has been a topic of discussion for centuries. Philosophers have considered objective, independent time and the relationship between time and causality.

Immanuel Kant, a leading philosopher, examined the concept of time and said that it forms the basic human cognitive system through which we structure our experiences. He argued that our understanding of time as a linear sequence of events is a human system of self-centered, innate consciousness. This thought experiment corresponds to the philosophical question of whether there is a natural sequence of time or whether it is merely an invention of our senses.

Without external reference points or conceptual systems such as clocks and calendars, it is difficult to assign a precise order or sequence to individual moments in time.

This means that the order and progression we perceive in time are products of our consciousness and are not necessarily reflective of the actual timing of natural phenomena. Overall, examples from physics and philosophy illustrate the idea that individual temporal units appear devoid of external structures and patterns, lacking any inherent structure or continuity. We rely on that structure to organize and understand the passage of time so that we can comprehend our experiences and interactions with the world. Perception of time is determined not only by the objective continuity of seconds, minutes, and hours but also by subjective experiences influenced by various factors, including continuous information. Engaging in absorbing activities and being emotionally sensitive can cause time to fly by, while boredom or a lack of engagement can make it seem to slow down. Context significantly shapes our perception of time. Engaging in stimulating conversations, events, or activities prompts our brains to process a plethora of novel information. Consequently, time appears to fly by as our minds remain fully engrossed, and our attention to external stimuli influences our temporal experience.

Conversely, environments characterized by limited sensory input or repetitive tasks can lead to a heightened awareness of time passing. In situations where sensory stimulation is lacking or tasks become monotonous, our brains may struggle to process new information, resulting in a sense of time slowing down.

For instance, waiting in an empty room or performing repetitive tasks can accentuate our perception of time due to the absence of external stimuli.

By acknowledging the influence of different contexts on our perception of time, we deepen our understanding of the intricate interplay between our environment and temporal experience. These examples vividly demonstrate the impact our surroundings have on our perception of time. In addition, our perception of time is closely connected to our memory. When we look at moments filled with memorable experiences, we realize that time passes quickly, while uneventful moments seem slower in retrospect. This exploration of the role of memory in our perception of time adds depth to our research. Strong emotions, such as joy and fear, can make time seem to fly by when our minds are preoccupied.

Conversely, negative emotions can make us more aware of the passing seconds, making us feel like time is slipping away. Our exploration of sensory experiences enhances the discussion of the subjective nature of discovering time. In the world of quantum physics, time plays an important role in how things change and evolve. It seems to be the key to governing the way quantum systems evolve and change.

Now, thanks to discoveries in quantum physics, we understand that our physical reality goes beyond what we can touch and see. There is a hidden aspect that is not physical in the traditional sense. Although we cannot see it directly, this invisible realm has an effect on the world we live in.

It is like the space behind the curtain where possibilities are born, and our experiences of those possibilities bear fruit in the things we encounter in our daily lives.

Recent discoveries suggest that these universal forces, which are not physical, have structures similar to our own thoughts and mental processes. This means that the universe works in an interconnected way, where everything is linked, and consciousness emerges as a universal aspect of existence. It is as if the universe itself has a kind of knowledge, a way of knowing the true self. However, the concept of a divine Creator explaining these mysteries remains disputed among modern scholars. While some readily accept the notion of a higher power, others remain skeptical, preferring to adhere strictly to empirical evidence and natural explanations. Yet evidence unearthed by quantum mechanics and cosmology hints at the necessity of a transcendent force or deity. From where does this supreme being, if it exists, derive its existence? The essence of things, as observed in the countless phenomena of the world, is characterized by their unique limitations and qualities. However, the mere existence of these entities transcends their essence.

They are animated by something outside of themselves, something that permeates them with reality. For example, the iPhone, the Mona Lisa or the humble potato - each has its own unique essence, but their existence depends on something beyond their intrinsic qualities. They exist, but they don't have to exist. Their temporality and limitation encourage us to think about the basic reasons for their existence. In a world full of transient phenomena, the question arises: why do these things exist at all?

The answer lies in the notion of a supreme being, a necessary existence whose essence encompasses existence itself. This transcendent entity serves as the anchor of reality, the underlying force that allows all other things to exist. While iPhones may one day disintegrate into recycled materials and works of art fade into obscurity, this supreme being remains the foundation of existence itself. Thinking about the necessity of a being whose essence is existence, we are confronted with the very essence of reality itself. It seems to remind us that the universe, in all its splendor and complexity, may ultimately be a reflection of something far greater, the divine essence from which all existence springs.

MANIFESTATION OF FORCE AND GRACE

Although we are very successful in the material world, we do not place much emphasis on spiritual wisdom. In this sense, we do not understand what gives individuals dignity and self-control in terms of their power, nature, and the world. Because of the spiritual environment in our time and the unrealistic demands on our time and attention, many of us yearn for the peace of the past. Temples, pyramids, churches, cathedrals, mosques, and other structures are symbols of deep wisdom and spiritual understanding. However, they are not the only ultimate goals; instead, they are vehicles for spiritual growth and enlightenment. These spaces are designed to cleanse, freshen, perfect, and elevate the mood of the passenger or service member. Similarly, the human body can have a similar transformative effect when engaged in spiritual practice or introspection, leading to personal growth and enlightenment. Essentially, sacred order and personal introspection are methods and means of spiritual growth and self-discovery.

Humanity can elevate Einstein's famous theory, often associated with scientific logic, to a quasi-sacred or revered status. This shows the importance and influence of Einstein's theory, commonly known as $E=mc^2$, transcends its science. Having gained respected status, this may indicate how widely accepted and culturally important Einstein's work is in our understanding of the universe and what his discoveries mean to human knowledge and the collective worldview.

So, what exactly do we know about the speed of light? The exact speed of light remains uncertain despite close approximations, prompting the need for a theory explaining its value and the universal speed limit. This uncertainty stems from factors such as the medium through which light travels. However, its speed in a vacuum, denoted by 'c', remains approximately 299,792,458 meters per second, a fundamental constant in physics. This raises questions about the relationship between the speed of light and the nature of light itself, as well as what makes it special among other phenomena. The universe does not intentionally set the speed of light but emerges naturally from the fundamental properties of electromagnetism and spacetime.

While spacetime itself is indifferent to light, the speed of light serves as a universal speed limit, extending to the concept of the speed of causality. In simpler terms, this limit defines how events influence each other in the universe, with light traveling at its inherent maximum speed, serving as a fundamental parameter in the fabric of spacetime.

There was a time when the prevailing notion embraced the somewhat disheartening idea that reality unfolds like a deterministic program.

The famous double-slit experiment, involving the scattering of electrons, decisively refuted determinism. For those unfamiliar, exploring the remarkable double-slit experiment in modern physics is crucial; it's a cornerstone of the field. This experiment has paved the way for a new era of non-determinism, introducing a concept akin to free will.

But how exactly does free will work? Quantum physics uncovers an insight: reality comes into existence solely through observation. In the most fundamental sense, particles materialize only upon being observed. The renowned physicist John Wheeler, who coined the term 'black hole," believes that reality is information created by a conscious observer. Nobel laureate Frank Wilczek acknowledges the complicated nature of quantum theory and suggests that until an observer is modeled within quantum mechanics, there will be mysteries. Wilczek speaks of an entity that is capable of generating information through observation, and that does not necessarily have to be a human or an animal. If reality is indeed made up of pure information, encompassing everything from energy to thought, it becomes clear that it is closely linked to consciousness.

Imagine a world in which free will operates within the framework of quantum mechanics as defined by some interpretations of the theory. In this hypothetical scenario:

Quantum Superposition: Objects, including particles and large systems, can exist in multiple states simultaneously until detected or measured. This superposition allows for multiple possible outcomes or alternatives.

Observer Effect: The act of observing or measuring causes the quantum state to collapse into a particular outcome within a certain range. This collapse occurs due to the interaction between the observed system and the measuring instrument, which may involve live observers.

Free Will and Observation: Free will manifests as the ability of conscious beings to influence the outcome of quantum phenomena through their observations and choices. Individual choices can affect the probability of an outcome and therefore subtly shape reality.

Consciousness and Reality: In this fictional setting, consciousness is intricately intertwined with the essence of reality. The conscious awareness of the observer plays a crucial role in determining the concrete results of quantum phenomena, thus shaping the observed reality.

This raises the question: Did consciousness and information evolve in a feedback loop?

Scientists agree that there is a fundamental limit to length, known as the Planck length, which implies a pixelated nature of reality. Skepticism about the concept of pixelation may stem from an aversion to this notion. We expect clarification with the advent of a theory of quantum gravity that explains pixelated spacetime. Scientists use sophisticated tools such as the Large Hadron Collider to study the tiniest building blocks of the universe called fundamental particles, along with the forces that control them. These particles and forces follow specific rules known as gauge symmetry.

An interesting idea in this study was the discovery of an eight-dimensional structure called the E8 lattice, which acts as a sort of structure for the universe. This lattice provides a framework for understanding spatial arrangements, even though it exists in dimensions beyond our direct perception.

To grasp the complexity of this structure, scientists project the eight-dimensional lattice multiple times to create a three-dimensional pattern known as a quasicrystal. It's like taking something from a higher-dimensional space and translating it into a form we can comprehend in our three-dimensional world. The shape of this lattice called the Gosset polytope is akin to a cube for a regular three-dimensional lattice. It serves as a fundamental unit of the E8 lattice and helps us simplify the understanding of its structure. When projected onto a four-dimensional space, the shape divides into two identical forms of different sizes, following a size ratio of 0.618, known as the reciprocal of the golden ratio. This ratio, believed to be a fundamental constant, appears widely across the universe, from the smallest particles in quantum physics to massive celestial bodies and even within black holes. Think of energy as some expression of the ability of particles to rotate or interact with their surroundings. Think of them as possibilities.

Now when we talk about reality, it seems that it should have a geometric shape or structure. This means that we can have unique languages or symbols based on concepts to help us better understand and communicate reality. In a geometric sense, these symbols can represent reality in unique ways, show how things interact, and even represent each other.

Geometric symbols are visual images that communicate the concepts of shape, symmetry, dimensionality, and properties of entities. The idea of a geometry-based language raises interesting questions: does such a language exist, and if so, what information would it express?

Specifically, a geometry-based language will use geometric symbols to express complex shapes and concepts. Just as words express meaning in spoken languages, geometric symbols are the building blocks of this unique language, communicating complex mathematical conceptual relationships. For example, geometric shapes, faces, and structures can represent abstract concepts such as symmetry, proportion, balance, and structure.

The sequence and combination of these symbols can reveal relationships between objects and events in the world. Could it be a language or code that only contains geometry? If so, what information would such a language reveal?

A geometric structure can express mathematical concepts or physical laws, while relationships between geometric symbols can express logical connections or mathematical operations. Modifying and interpreting these symbols can make it possible to speak geometrically, especially when communicating complex ideas. Symbols are the foundation of knowledge that existed before we understood the world. They express aspects of reality that cannot be achieved in non-figurative language because of their inherent subjectivity and value. Symbolism originally evolved through sensory experiences, allowing people to transcend empirical reality and reach a deeper understanding. Symbols define the world order, establish social relations, ensure continuous culture, and guide individuals to interpret the picture of the world. It contains valuable information that helps us understand the world.

Many physicists see symbols as the basic building blocks of our reality. However, there are contradictions. Critics of the idea that reality is information attempt to define what reality is by examining its basic characteristics, seeking to uncover its essence beyond the conceptual framework of information theory.

The concept that reality is composed of information, as suggested by both quantum and classical physics, can affect our thoughts about self-awareness. First, it challenges traditional notions of the self as a separate and isolated entity by suggesting that individual consciousness and awareness are intricately connected to the essence of reality itself. The concept that reality is fundamentally built on information suggests that our consciousness and self-awareness may be integral components of this information framework.

Additionally, if reality is shaped by observation and perception, as quantum mechanics implies, then our individual consciousness can play a significant role in shaping the reality we experience. This term implies a dynamic interplay between the observer and the observed, whereby self-awareness affects the very structure of reality. Moreover, the idea that reality is composed of pure information implies a deep interconnectedness of all things, which extends beyond individual boundaries. This interconnectedness suggests that our sense of self-awareness is intertwined with the larger framework of existence. Thinking about the relationship between self-awareness and the informational nature of reality prompts a rethinking of our understanding of consciousness, perception, and the fundamental nature of existence.

I am certainly aware of the implications of our consciousness in shaping the world around us and defining our place in it. But what if reality is the independent nature and existence of all that is known, whether known through logical reasoning, empirical observation, or some other form of experience? The existence and nature of reality are independent because reality does not depend on how well our minds understand it to continue to exist or to retain its character.

TIMELESS NEANDERTHAL SHADOWS

The human heart contains approximately 40,000 stem cells. Inside the heart resides a nerve that sends more information to the brain than vice versa. This means that the heart-brain interface is more active than the brain-heart interface. Electrically, the heart boasts 5,000 times the strength of the brain, and its electric field extends over a distance of 2-8 meters. As one engages and connects, their heart intelligence facilitates full presence, connection, and guidance with the heart in all aspects of life, resulting in higher creative experiences and performance.

Within our hearts lies the wisdom to guide us toward decisions that bring happiness and success. Relying solely on our 'master brain' greatly undermines this wisdom, leading to confusion and stagnation.

Modern society often leaves us feeling stuck and looking for external solutions. Skills, input, creative thinking, self-esteem, and optimism stem from motivation and problem-solving abilities. The parallels between the human heart and brain are indeed interesting and significant. Just as the heart has thousands of muscle cells and its nervous system, the brain has millions of nerve connections that are fundamental to the optimal functioning of the body and overall well-being. Furthermore, the dynamic interaction between the heart and the brain highlights the complexity of human physiology.

While primarily recognized as a pump, the heart is a sophisticated information-processing center, with an extensive nervous system that facilitates two-way communication with the brain. This transmission of vital signals greatly affects the emotional and cognitive aspects.

Like the heart's powerful electrical impulses, the brain generates complex electrical activities that underlie cognitive processes and cognition. Both organs exhibit remarkable electrical activity, revealing the intricate pathways of neurons and signalling. Additionally, just as engaging the intelligence of the heart can enhance presence and guide decision-making, tapping into the brain's vast reservoir of muscle can enable creativity, problem-solving, and coping with emotions.

The discovery of the striking similarities between the heart and the brain highlights the homogeneity of human physiology and emphasizes the importance of managing overall well-being through the promotion of physical and mental health. As we seek to develop a deeper understanding of ourselves and harness our innate abilities, embracing the innate wisdom of the heart and brain can empower us to live fulfilling and authentic lives.

Imagine your brain as a huge network of connections, similar to a complex network of neurons. When these neurons fire and make connections, they generate what we call information. This information serves as the foundation that helps your brain understand the world around you and make sense of your experiences.

According to Integrated Information Theory (IIT), your brain does not process information randomly. Instead, it is structured so that the information it generates is integrated, meaning that it is interconnected and influences each other. This integrated information leads to your conscious experiences , your thoughts, feelings, and perceptions. Think of it like this: When different regions of your brain communicate and work together, they create a diverse landscape of experiences. These experiences are not simply made up of isolated pieces of information, but result from the intricate interactions and connections between these elements.

The more integrated and interconnected this information is in your brain, the more conscious and aware you become of your decisions and actions. So when you make a conscious decision, your brain draws on a vast network of interconnected concepts, beliefs, memories, and desires. This complex network gives meaning to your decisions and makes you feel in control of your actions. Simply put, IIT helps us understand how our brains process information to shape our conscious experiences, and how the complexity of this information network influences our sense of free will and consciousness.

It would indeed be remarkable if we could get our brains to store only positive, happy, and sunny information. Such an ability would allow us to maintain a constant sense of well-being and positivity. Unfortunately, we have not yet reached that point.

Now, after every positive event in my life, I find myself in a unique ritual of reflection. As I reflect back on the depths of my past, confronting every challenge and reliving each loss, I undergo a significant transformation, a fundamental shift in my perspective emerges from these moments. At that moment, the weight of past struggles was lifted, freeing me from their merciless grip and weakening their dominance over my existence. This moment becomes a serious testimony to the sovereignty I have over my destiny. I am no longer just an observer of life's unfolding drama; I am an active participant, a sculptor who shapes the contours of my reality.

Standing on the edge of every new opportunity, I look at the past as fertile ground from which my future narratives spring, and I, the author, get to tell my life stories. This realization provokes a deep meditation on the mysterious dance between existence and emptiness, leading me through the labyrinth of being. At every moment, I find myself at the crossroads of history and the present, tightly gripped by the reins of destiny. This revelation resonates within me, lighting a flame of empowerment that defies the shackles of time. With this enlightenment, the search for external recognition diminishes in importance. I emerge as the master of my positivity, strengthened by the indomitable strength that lives deep within me. The world turns into a huge canvas on which I sketch the vivid shades of my intentions and aspirations. Every decision becomes a move of my creative agency, creating a life imbued with purposeful determination and unyielding faith.

RARE GLIMPSE OF THE ELUSIVE

In the depths of the human soul rages a stormy conflict, an eternal struggle between the forces of light and darkness, virtue and vice. I can entertain abstract thoughts, recall my experiences, and question reality. This grants me the freedom to create, understand better, and communicate with others, unlike other animals. However, it also makes me aware of my limitations and the fact that I will eventually die, understanding that my time here is finite.

Although wrestling with these weighty matters can be challenging, it also helps me appreciate the world around me. It enables me to forge meaningful relationships and find purpose in life, which is fundamental to my human experience. I underwent significant transformations when I began contemplating death and consciousness. I moved away from simplistic thinking and confronted the difficult questions of life and death, seeking deeper meaning.

Contemplating death should guide me to explore the meaning of life. This concept is reflected in ancient stories where individuals plummet from the sky, symbolizing people's attempts to find significance in life after realizing their mortality. While contemplating these questions can be daunting, they ultimately help me discover purpose and connect with others in a meaningful way. Think of my mind as a vast open space where ideas come and go randomly. It's like a room where ideas flow uninterrupted.

But here's the tricky part: even though I can think and have thoughts in my mind, I can't see where these thoughts come from or how my mind forms them. It's kind of peculiar when I think about it. I may perceive that my mind is brimming with thoughts, but I cannot discern where they originate or how they materialize. The source of my thoughts is invisible; that's how my mind operates.

I only become aware of it when a thought materializes in my mind and I contemplate it. Thoughts that don't distract me come and go quickly, leaving no trace. So essentially, my mind is like a big mystery box where ideas appear and disappear, but I don't always know their origin or how they emerge. This is one of those things that is both exciting and slightly perplexing to my mind at the same time. If there were something outside of me that gave me ideas, I could see where they came from.

But the real nature of thinking is still a mystery to me. Even the deepest thoughts don't leave a clear sign in my mind, like light rays passing through a vast thinking space. Remembering this is important. Let's connect this line of thought with creativity and the perception of ideas. Initially, my mind is flooded with numerous ideas. However, with reduced mental engagement, multiple ideas coalesce into a single concept. A continuous decrease in my mental activity diminishes the clarity of these ideas.

As I distance myself from the origin of these ideas, they become more obscure and eventually disappear from view altogether. This analogy extends to the different ways in which I interpret and understand concepts.

My mind, especially if I am very perceptive, is more open to new ideas compared to the average mind. This means I can notice things others might miss. If I am far away from what inspires me, I still maintain some awareness of it. In this situation, something interesting happens: inspiration shows up at different times as I mentally move further away. The farther I go, the longer it takes for inspiration to show up again. Imagine an experienced chef and me preparing a meal together in a busy kitchen.

The experienced chef, who has a flair for the nuances of flavors and textures, effortlessly weaves the ingredients together, guided by intuition and experience. With each culinary creation, the chef's mind becomes fertile ground for creativity. Additionally, I, as a novice cook, who is equally enthusiastic but lacks culinary wisdom, experience fleeting moments of inspiration. I may try to emulate the chef's techniques, but my culinary landscape is not as rich and finely tuned. As the two of us continue our culinary journey, the experienced chef's mind picks up inspiration at irregular intervals and remains connected to the essence of cooking regardless of the challenges. Even as we explore new recipes and techniques, the chef's connection to culinary inspiration remains steadfast. In contrast, I, as a novice cook who is not as familiar with the intricacies of cooking, may find that the gaps between moments of inspiration increase, and my connection to the culinary art becomes more tenuous as I try my hand at more complex dishes. This example illustrates how the receptivity of the human mind, especially that of an experienced person, can substantially affect the experience and manifestation of inspiration in various creative endeavors.

In the mind, ideas pulse like flashes of inspiration, each one sounding as vivid as the next, regardless of the mental distance that separates them.

This phenomenon highlights a fundamental limit to the spread of ideas and demonstrates that they retain their power even amidst countless thoughts. Consider this: every flash of inspiration that a thinker experiences arises from a mental spark that ignites their consciousness. Interestingly, these sparks do not diminish with distance, but the mental landscape between them seems to darken as space increases. If the mind has difficulty grasping an idea, it is not because the ideas themselves are weak, but because they cannot penetrate the consciousness of the mind. This fascinating property is similar to quantization, a concept familiar in quantum theory. Here, each fragment of thought, each idea, functions as a mental quantum, a discrete unit of intellectual energy.

The essence of quantum theory reflects this property and extends its application to all measurable mental quantities in the field of creative thinking. It posits that the intellectual landscape is not continuous but consists of discrete, infinitely divisible mental quanta, each contributing to the rich mosaic of human thought. Quantization in quantum theory is a concept that describes how certain properties, such as energy or momentum, can only exist in specific, discrete amounts or "chunks". It's a bit like how you can only buy whole apples at the grocery store, not apple parts. In quantum theory, things like energy and momentum are broken down into these indivisible units called quanta.

Think of it as if the universe has a set of building blocks, and everything from light to matter is made up of these tiny, fundamental units. This idea was a major advance in physics because it helped scientists understand the behavior of particles at the smallest scales, such as those inside atoms.

Quantization also plays a key role in explaining how light behaves as both particles and waves and forms the basis of many modern technologies, such as lasers and semiconductors. So, simply put, quantization is the idea that certain properties of particles come in discrete, specific amounts, rather than being continuous.

Thus, the pulsating nature of ideas in the mind, regardless of their spatial separation, underscores a fundamental aspect of human cognition: the enduring power of inspiration amid the complexity of thought. Each flash of insight, similar to a mental spark, retains its vitality at various distances within the landscape of the mind, suggesting the depth of the creative process. This intriguing property finds resonance with the concept of quantization in quantum theory.

Within this framework, each fragment of thought, each idea, functions as a discrete unit of intellectual energy, a mental quantum. This notion reflects the basic principles of quantum theory and extends its applicability to the field of human cognition. By positing that the intellectual field comprises discrete, infinitely divisible mental quanta, quantum theory sheds light on the intricate mosaic of human thought and creativity.

Quantization, as explained in quantum theory, describes how certain properties of particles, such as energy and momentum, exist only in specific, indivisible quantities or "chunks". This concept, akin to buying whole apples instead of fractions, has revolutionized our understanding of particle behavior at the smallest scales, offering deep insight into the nature of matter and energy. Moreover, quantization serves as a cornerstone in explaining phenomena such as the dual nature of light and underpins the development of modern technologies such as lasers and semiconductors. Essentially, quantization reveals that certain properties of particles manifest themselves in discrete, precise quantities, a key concept that shapes our understanding of the universe at its most fundamental level.

A GARDEN FOR ORPHEUS

An idea represents a concept or thought that may or may not be grounded in fact. A belief is a conviction I hold to be true, even in the absence of evidence. An interpretation reflects my understanding or explanation of something, influenced by my beliefs and ideas. A scientific fact is a proposition repeatedly tested and validated through scientific experimentation and observation, rooted in evidence, and acknowledged as true within the current scientific understanding. The distinction between living and non-living entities relies on specific characteristics such as the capacity for growth, reproduction, and maintenance of homeostasis, rather than the presence of a non-physical element like a soul.

These defining characteristics delineate life and are observable in living organisms, while non-living entities lack them. The concept of a soul or anima remains a belief specific to certain cultures and religions, lacking scientific substantiation. Regarding my conscious mind and its influence on my movements, if my particles adhere to the laws of physics, the soul's involvement becomes irrelevant. Conversely, if my particles deviate from known physical laws due to the soul's influence, the soul can be viewed as just another physical entity capable of exerting forces on particles. This perspective aligns with how physicists historically approached new fields of forces and particles. Humanistically, empirical knowledge cannot equate to "wisdom" and scarcely comprehends the human experience. Empirical knowledge, while valuable, falls short in capturing the depth and complexity of human existence.

Wisdom, encompassing more than factual knowledge, integrates experience, intuition, and empathy to make sound judgments. Empirical knowledge, limited to observation and analysis of specific phenomena, cannot fully grasp the complexity of humanity. Usually, there is the other side of the same coin, acknowledging that my world may not be suitable for the human mind reflects a subjective viewpoint.

Some individuals perceive the world as too complex or chaotic for full comprehension, while others believe in the adaptability and growth of the human mind in various environments. Despite challenges, humans have historically thrived in diverse conditions, demonstrating the mind's capacity for understanding, problem-solving, creativity, and innovation.

Challenges in navigating my world can be addressed through personal development, self-care, therapy, community support, and social and political activism. In essence, I inhabit a system that may pose challenges to my human mind yet remains fertile ground for growth, adaptation, and exploration. In my pursuit of self-awareness, I explore various fields spanning the spectrum of human understanding. From the abstract concepts of science to the precise logic of mathematics, from the introspective realms of philosophy to the expansive vistas of physics, and from the sacred depths of religion to existential contemplations, I traverse the landscape of knowledge with an insatiable hunger for insight. Scientific concepts, like religious beliefs, are constructs of the human mind; without human interpretation, they lack significance.

The idea that humans impose laws upon nature resonates more strongly than the reverse notion; that nature imposes laws upon humans. As I attribute meaning to scientific concepts that come from the depths of my mind, subjective influence assumes a key role. Without my subjective influence, these concepts would not undergo metamorphosis, would lose their luster, and fade like an echo in space. In this context, subjective interpretation becomes inseparable from objective understanding, shaping the essence of scientific concepts and human understanding. I consciously identify as a rational architect molding reality by imposing laws on the natural order, a notion congruent with the symphony of reason rather than the discord of chance.

Transitioning to mathematics, my pursuit transcends mere problem-solving; it becomes a delicate act of creation. Proving theorems, akin to intellectual ballets, demands a harmonious interplay of logic, intricately weaving patterns that connect newfound truths to existing knowledge structures. Philosophy, infused with vibrant ideas, dedicates itself to meticulous logical examination, crafting arguments resilient to scrutiny's tempest. In the annals of physics, resembling a detective story, I endeavor to unravel the cosmos' mysteries. Theories, rooted in informed conjecture, serve as adaptable tools, flexing to accommodate understanding rather than rigid dogma. Through experimentation, research, and the language of mathematics, I engage in an unyielding pursuit, each endeavor deepening comprehension. Religion, an ethereal realm untouched by empirical evidence or logical rigor, beckons me on a personal journey of faith and cultural identity.

The myriad faiths, resembling a kaleidoscope of human spirituality, emphasize the heart's ineffable sentiments over empirical confirmation's rigorous demands.

So, who is lying: Nature or Man? In a constant search for knowledge and personal insight, I navigate different intellectual fields, each of which governs its own particular rules and aesthetics. This Iliad unfolds as a metaphorical narrative, revealing the inherent variety, difference, and connectedness in my unjust quest to understand the world. Unfair for the reason that I am aware of the magnitude of this undertaking. Imagine a reality where interchangeability underscores the shared unity within human understanding. Imagine a world where the concept of substitutability unites individual perceptions and interpretations in the scientific, mathematical, philosophical, and religious domains.

As I walk this expansive intellectual field, I recognize interchangeability as an ethereal key, seamlessly linking various forms of thought into a coherent understanding. In my human experience, art appears as a synthesis of intellectual pursuits, abstract scientific concepts, mathematical theorems, philosophical musings, and the spiritual insights of religion.

These threads intertwine, finding resonance through interpretive thought and subjective influence, giving artistic expressions depth and significance. Art asserts itself boldly, akin to the sensual architecture that shapes my emotional and cultural reality. Through harmonious compositions of shape, color, and form, art resonates with emotions and perceptions, building unique aesthetic knowledge.

Dedicated to exploration and expression, art offers visual and auditory narratives open to different interpretations, delving into life's mysteries and fundamental forces. Its myriad expressions serve as a kaleidoscope that reflects my human spirituality, inviting personal introspection of identity and emotion. Thus, in a world full of abundance, art takes on the role of metaphorical narrative on the cognitive stage, an exploration that illuminates the diversity inherent in my quest for understanding. Through the exploration of intellectual domains, art is transformed into a narrative that emphasizes the intricacies of navigating the complexity of the world. Art, in its various expressions, embodies an interchangeability, a shared essence in the understanding of humanity.

By dealing with scientific concepts, mathematics, philosophy, physics, religion, and art itself, I unravel the intricate interactions of ideas that characterize each domain. In this framework, art acts as a bridge, effortlessly linking different forms of thought into a cohesive understanding. In my exploration of art and its integration with different fields of knowledge, I aim to deepen my understanding of the human condition.

Art serves as a unifying force, connecting different domains and contributing to a multifaceted understanding of humanity's collective development. As an artist, I see human behavior as deeply influenced by environment rather than innate characteristics. This perspective shapes my artistic approach, where I challenge classic images and create compositions with ambiguous content.

By blurring the lines between subject and presentation, I seek to underline the influence of the environment on human perception. This approach invites me and you, the viewer, to think about the complexity of the art world and the subtle interplay between context and interpretation. I often surrender to the truth, perhaps in which I only believe that Beauty, inherently subjective, defies precise explanation, but comes to the fore through art.

An objective perception of art can evoke an aesthetic sensibility, bridging personal experiences with shared emotions. I recognize the influence of material goods, time, and space on my thoughts, anchoring my artistic expression in the principle of "internal necessity." Emotionally resonant impressions find form in art, erasing the boundaries between formal structure and basic content. Contemporary art is increasingly exploring themes of personal identity in the digital age, reflecting on the transformative impact of technology and the Internet. Through the creation of alter-egos and the manipulation of self-representation, artists tap into the flexibility and instability of the modern self.

These investigations illuminate the evolving nature of identity and invite contemplation of the intersection of technology, perception, and self-awareness. The integration of technology into human life has ushered in a transformative paradigm of identity, as posited by scholars such as Sherry Turkle and Paul B. Preciado.

This new perspective blurs conventional distinctions between man and machine, male and female, subject and object, and authentic and artificial.

The human being is now perceived as a composite of particles, bits, pixels, genes, DNA structures, prosthetic devices, virtual projections, synthetic hormones, and more. Identity, gender, and sexuality are seen as synthetic, malleable, changeable, and technically produced and reproduced. In this cultural milieu, the demarcations between real and virtual, organic and inorganic, original and copy are rapidly dissolving.

Jean Baudrillard's concept of the simulacrum becomes relevant, suggesting that our understanding of reality is increasingly shaped by representations and simulations rather than reality itself. Similarly, Donna Haraway's notion of the cyborg, articulated in her seminal work "The Cyborg Manifesto" in 1985, echoes this sentiment, emphasizing the porous boundaries between human and machine. Both theorists argue that we exist as fully mediated beings in fully mediated worlds, leading to a re-understanding of the self marked by multiplicity, heterogeneity, flexibility, and fragmentation. Technological and medical advances further underscore this idea, facilitating the reproduction of bodies and blurring the lines between the real and the virtual. Internet technology has revolutionized the distribution of memory, significantly transforming communication.

Social media platforms, digital archives, and online journals now serve as repositories for our collective experiences, shaping our understanding of reality. However, it is important to recognize that memories stored digitally do not always guarantee authenticity. Despite advances in data storage, biases and limitations in digital archiving systems can compromise the integrity of memory.

The integration of technology into human life has fundamentally changed notions of identity, memory, and reality. It is imperative to critically examine the implications of these changes and consider how they reshape our understanding of ourselves and the world around us. In the complexities of digital encounters, we are often drawn to share extraordinary moments, but the elusive essence of authenticity permeates our understanding in this digital world.

The ephemeral nature of viral phenomena, as fascinating as they are, tempts us to ponder the authenticity they embody and the reality they shape. As we walk through this digital expanse, the notion of identity undergoes a metamorphosis, evolving through an intricate interplay of external influences and internal reflections. Once conceived as static, identity now develops as a dynamic interweaving of changing currents within our environment.

 By drawing parallels between our contemporary digital milieu and the ancient wisdom of Eastern philosophies and shamanic traditions, we gain insight into the essence of identity. In the teachings of Buddhism and Taoism, as well as in shamanic rites, identity appears as a fluid construct, intricately intertwined with a universal essence that transcends individual boundaries. Concepts such as Anata and Tao emphasize the transcendent nature of identity, highlighting its essential connection to the fabric of existence. Similarly, the Yoga Sutras explain the interconnectedness of the individual soul with the universal soul, encouraging practitioners to embark on a journey of self-realization through contemplation and introspection.

Indigenous wisdom traditions reflect these sentiments, extolling the unity of all life forms and the imperative of harmonious coexistence with nature, transmitted through ancient rituals and shared stories. Juxtaposing the wisdom of antiquity with the complexity of our digital age, we are compelled to contemplate identity as a dynamic phenomenon shaped by external stimuli and internal introspection. Just as ancient doctrines recognize identity as a reflection of a universal essence, the digital age presents identity as a multifaceted interaction between our digital selves and tangible reality. It prompts us to explore the depths of authenticity in a realm where perceptions can be shaped at the push of a button. We are invited to reflect on our digital interactions and their impact on our sense of self. How do these virtual engagements shape our identity?

How can we strike a balance between the virtual and the tangible, the authentic and the fictional? These explorations beckon us to embark on an odyssey of self-discovery, uncovering deep truths that connect us in our shared quest for enlightenment.

ART COLLECTION: A GARDEN FOR ORPHEUS

In a space where beauty stands as an inherently subjective concept, intangible and resistant to conveyance, a compelling exploration unfolds at the crossroads of personal perception and shared understanding. Art emerges as a medium adept at bridging the chasm, translating the subtleties of individual aesthetic senses into a universally comprehensible language. For ZT Tosha, the conviction in the deep influence of material possessions, time, and space on thought processes serves as a guiding principle. The acknowledgment that these realities mold their cognitive landscape leads to a realization, thinking is inseparable from these tangible elements. Yet, within this intricate interplay, the vastness of infinite time and space, while shaping thoughts, remains unseen and elusive. Driven by the principle of "internal necessity," ZT Tosha creates their artwork as a direct response to inner experiences. These inner echoes, which emotionally reverberate with the external world, undergo a transformative process, morphing into symbols that carry profound meaning and rich information. If these symbols are then presented objectively as images, they wield the ability to elicit aesthetic emotions in the viewer, creating a fusion that blurs the boundaries between the artist's personal world and the shared experience of those who perceive the art. In essence, the artwork becomes a conduit through which personal emotions and universally relatable sentiments intertwine, creating a bridge between the intimate and the collective.

As the narrative unfolds, the story broadens its perspective on testimony and witnessing in the digital age. The ubiquity of cell phones and miniature cameras becomes a pervasive tool, empowering individuals not only to assert, "I was there; this is what I saw," but to collectively bear witness through media. The cell phone, especially, takes center stage, casting the audience as both the ultimate addressee and primary producer. It transforms the collective into the subject and object of everyday witnessing, capturing and testifying to its own historical reality as it unfolds. In this exploration of perception, art, and technology, the story navigates the ambiguity between the formal framework of images and their content.

It delves into how individuals, armed with the tools of witnessing, contribute to the collective narrative, intertwining personal experiences with the shared historical reality. "Shadows of Perception" weaves together the threads of beauty, artistic expression, and digital witnessing into a narrative that transcends the boundaries of the personal and the collective.

SHAPING ART THROUGH TIME

The essence of Schopenhauer's philosophy provides a deep lens through which we can see the fundamental layers of artistic creation. In this framework, we witness the fusion of subjective desires, encapsulated in the concept of Will, with the external form and expression of works of art, thus making them manifestations of Ideas. This sharing of the artist's inner world and external manifestations serves as a channel for deciphering intentions and inviting viewers to journeys of subjective and rational interpretation.

Looking back at the history of art, Schopenhauer's philosophy offers a background for the evolution of art movements. In the era of the Renaissance, exemplified by Raphael's "School of Athens", artists not only sought to capture the external world, but also plunged into the realm of the human spirit, embodying the fusion of will and representation. Delving into individual works of art such as Raphael's 'School of Athens', it becomes apparent how composition and symbolism reflect Schopenhauer's notion of will and representation. By exploring the subtle nuances within the painting, viewers can discern the artist's reflections on philosophical ideals and the human condition. Moreover, by analyzing this symbolism and the innovative techniques used by artists such as Hieronymus Bosch in The Garden of Earthly Delights, readers gain insight into the multiple interpretations of Schopenhauer's philosophy within the context of Surrealism.

Bosch's vivid portrayal of human desire and the consequences of enjoyment invites rational engagement with deeper meanings, while reflecting a world driven by human desire and change.

Confronting the perennial tension between subjectivity and objectivity, artworks such as Picasso's 'Les Demoiselles d'Avignon' question conventional representations by echoing the world as Will - a departure from the ordinary, an exploration of change and fluidity that reveals the transformative nature of art. By dissecting the cubist elements and underlying themes of Picasso's masterpiece, readers can discern Schopenhauer's influence on the artist's deconstruction of form and reality, thus inviting the contemplation of subjective interpretations. Edvard Munch's The Scream poignantly portrays existential turmoil, depicting human emotions and anxieties amidst a turbulent landscape – a vivid depiction of Schopenhauer's philosophy that embraces the raw and emotional dimensions of human life. By examining the expressive techniques and psychological depths of Munch's work, readers gain insight into the artist's exploration of universal human experiences, echoing Schopenhauer's emphasis on the primacy of the individual will. In contemporary art, artists like

ZT Tosha engage with Schopenhauer's philosophical concepts, using technology to explore the subjective, dynamic nature of human experience. Through digital media, they enter the realm of the will, creating immersive experiences that combine sensory input and evoke emotional responses, reminiscent of Schopenhauer's view of a world driven by human desire.

Technological innovations are redefining artistic representation, enabling the precise display of complex emotions and ideas. The works of ZT Toša represent an example of the interchangeability of will and representation, where subjective experiences intertwine with rational and symbolic interpretations. It is necessary to acknowledge and respond to potential criticisms or alternative interpretations of Schopenhauer's philosophy and its influence on art.

While Schopenhauer's philosophy offers profound insight into the nature of artistic creation, it also provokes debate about the extent of its influence and applicability in different artistic contexts. By engaging with different perspectives, readers can develop a more nuanced understanding of the complexities inherent in the relationship between philosophy and art. The enduring influence of Schopenhauer's philosophy on art underscores the timeless relevance of philosophical inquiry in shaping human expression and perception. By exploring the intersection of Schopenhauer's ideas with various artistic movements and individual works of art, we gain a deeper appreciation of the connection between philosophy and art throughout history. Through continued dialogue and research, we can further illuminate the transformative power of artistic creation in reflecting and shaping our understanding of the human experience.

ZT TOSHA: A QUIET REVOLUTION IN ART

ZT Tosha, born Zoran Tošić, is a prominent artist whose influence on the world art scene has reverberated since the late 1990s. Originally from Yugoslavia and currently residing in The Netherlands, Tosha is an example of the transformative potential of creativity. His art delicately transcends the complexities of human existence and our evolving environment. Through a meticulous exploration of form and content, he seamlessly interweaves classic images with textured frames, blurring the lines between reality and perception. Characterized by the relentless passage of time and the intricate interplay of personal beliefs and social norms, his oeuvre evokes a deep sense of introspection. In his own words, "A work of art will constantly remain torn between past judgments and present propositions if it cannot be permanently separated from them." This sentiment encapsulates Tosha's firm commitment to the dialogue between tradition and innovation.

Born in the midst of dynamic cultural changes in Yugoslavia in 1961, ZT Tosha draws inspiration from the vibrant energy of the 1990s, marked by the rise of global capitalism and the dawn of mass media. Immersed in the cultural currents of electronic pop music and hip-hop, his artistic vision reflects a diverse array of influences. The 1980s saw the emergence of avant-garde art movements such as Neo-Geo, The Pictures Generation and Neo-Expressionism, led by luminaries such as Anselm Kiefer, Joerg Immendorff and Jean-Michel Basquiat.

Their revolutionary contribution reshaped cultural discourse and left an indelible mark on the world of art. For ZT Tosha, the echoes of this transformative era and the towering artistic figures before him resonate in his work, infusing his creations with a delicate balance of nostalgia and innovation. His art transcends time constraints, offering viewers a path to introspection and exploration.

 In a world characterized by relentless progress, ZT Tosha's work stands as a symbol of artistic integrity and innovation, encouraging us to bravely and creatively face life's intricacies. Through his visionary art, he emphasizes that true greatness comes from the pursuit of authenticity and self-expression, not conformity.

THE PARADOX OF EXISTENCE

Imagine the vast expanse of the universe as a grand stage where particles engage in an intricate dance, gracefully transitioning between different states of energy. Unlike people, these particles do not succumb to the ravages of time or the burden of aging. Instead, they embody a timeless elegance as they shift and transform, shaping the very fabric of reality itself.

Now, picture yourself as a creator on this cosmic stage, harnessing the energy of these particles to sculpt and mold the world around you. Every thought, every action, every creation is fueled by this borrowed energy, allowing you to imprint your existence upon the universe, if only for a fleeting moment. But here lies the paradox: for the world to exist in the form you perceive it, your existence must precede it. Your consciousness, your very essence, is intimately intertwined with the essence of reality. You are not merely an observer, but an active participant in the ongoing creation of the cosmos.

Despite the ever-shifting landscape of your experiences - the ebb and flow of emotions, perceptions, and actions - there exists within you a core essence that remains unchanging. This essence is the bedrock of your identity, the immutable foundation upon which the edifice of your being is built. Consider, for instance, the feeling of love that envelops you when you are in the presence of those you hold dear.

Though circumstances may change, the essence of love remains a constant, a guiding light amidst life's uncertainties. Or reflect on the sense of purpose that drives you forward, propelling you to pursue your dreams and aspirations. This sense of purpose emanates from the core of your being, a steadfast beacon in the tumult of existence.

In essence, this core of your personality serves as an anchor, grounding you amidst the swirling currents of life. It is the essence of your being, the nucleus around which your experiences orbit. And though it may be difficult to articulate or define, it grants you a profound sense of certainty - a knowing that, no matter the trials and tribulations you may face, you remain true to yourself, steadfast in your essence.

EPILOGUE

 It is neither a miracle nor a secret that after this period of my linguistic research and expression, I stand on the edge of the unknown, humbled by the vast existence that stretches beyond the reach of words. My journey through the labyrinth of language has brought me face to face with enigmatic aspects of life that defy simple categorization. As I reflect on my quest for understanding, I realize that the limitations of language have become a catalyst for a deeper exploration of the human experience. In the silence between words, I find solace in acknowledging the inadequacy of language, accepting the inherent mystery that shrouds the unspeakable truths of existence.

With the guidance of respected thinkers and an introspective look into the recesses of my mind, I courageously undertook a quest of self-discovery. Each revelation, like a fragment of a mosaic, illuminates the essence of life, revealing the deep interaction of emotions, thoughts, and perceptions. Yet as I stand in the midst of uncertainty,

I recognize the resilience of the human spirit in the face of adversity. My search for truth continues, fueled by an unwavering determination to unravel the complexities of my innermost self and the world around me. Recalling my introspection, I accept doubt and curiosity as companions on the path to enlightenment. It is precisely through the unraveling of illusions that I glimpse the deep beauty of existence, transcending the boundaries of language to touch the essence of our common humanity.

And here we come to the end of the story written on the cover of my sketch pad. As I bid farewell to the Epilogue frame, let me thank you for reading these, my most precious thoughts, that define my existence.

ARTWORKS

REFLECTIONS OF SELF: EXPLORING THE INTERSECTION OF SURREALISM AND DIGITAL INNOVATION

"The work of art will remain permanently torn between past judgments and present suggestions if it cannot separate itself from them permanently." ZT Tosha

It is through the lens of our beliefs and understanding of art that we create and appreciate works of art. Thus, it is this self-referential aspect of art that interests me, the reflection of internal conflict between formal composition and image content. The ambiguity within an image's composition expresses tension between memory and content, revealing how our circumstances shape our actions more than our internal traits.

What makes my art unique is its self-referential nature; it does not reference anything outside itself but rather focuses on the internal dynamics of the image. My work explores the unconscious and irrational. As society continues to evolve and change, my work remains a testament to the power and impact of self-referential art.

My creative process: 'Juxtaposed Surrealist Stitches and Pixelated Portals'

Drawing Phase: The creative journey kicks off with the artist sketching out a design. This drawing acts as the blueprint, setting the stage for the entire artwork.

Oil Painting Stage: My abstract paintings undergo continuous changes. I often remove, erase, then add colors, rotate the canvas horizontally and vertically, examining the canvas from all angles. My pictures often turn out completely different from what I planned. Although it may not appear so, I don't have a specific palette; I start with transparent colors. At the very beginning, I use Rembrandt's "underpainting" technique, and during the painting process, I become more experimental. Sometimes, the painting process itself takes two to three years. This period of time is due to the drying of paint layers.

Transformation Through Cutting: Here comes the intriguing twist. The completed oil paintings are sliced into smaller segments. This physical act of cutting introduces a dynamic element, breaking down the traditional canvas boundaries and adding a sense of movement and fragmentation to the artwork.

Collage Assembly: The cut-up pieces are meticulously arranged into a collage. This stage is where the physicality of the process truly shines, as I navigate through various compositions, experimenting with textures, shapes, and patterns, anything I can find to craft a visually captivating arrangement.

Photography: Once the collage is arranged to satisfaction, it's time to capture it through photography. This step preserves the intricate arrangement and allows for further manipulation in the digital realm.

Digital Editing: The final piece undergoes digital manipulation, where the photograph of the collage serves as the canvas for further exploration and enhancement. This digital phase introduces a contemporary twist to the artwork, enabling the artist to play with color balance, contrast, and other digital effects, enriching the overall visual experience.

Creation of One-of-a-Kind Digital Artwork: Through this meticulous process blending traditional techniques with digital innovation, a one-of-a-kind digital artwork emerges. It's a fusion of the timeless allure of oil painting and drawing with the dynamic possibilities of digital manipulation, resulting in a piece that resonates with both tradition and modernity.

POSTSCRIPT

In the domain of artistic creation, truth isn't a static, easily grasped concept awaiting discovery through mere observation. Instead, it emerges as a dynamic interplay of negotiation, discourse, and interpretation. Thus, any artistic commentary demands continual analysis and dialogue to approach an objective truth.

This perspective diverges markedly from Hegel's notion of history as the realization of a singular idea, which implies a predetermined endpoint. It also differs from the teleologies of Christianity and Marxist-Leninism, which assert a fixed purpose for historical unfolding.

Furthermore, it challenges the progressive dogma that once influenced Western modernism within the artistic sphere. Rather than envisioning art as a vehicle for advancing towards a predefined future of societal betterment, it suggests that truth in art is ever-evolving, shaped by ongoing negotiations and interpretations.